AT THE SPEED OF DARK

Gabriel Àkámọ́ is a Nigerian-British poet, actor, facilitator, and creative producer. He has worked with numerous organisations including Rich Mix, Roundhouse and WIRED Next Generation. He has been commissioned by institutions such as the Southbank Centre, St. Paul's Cathedral and the Royal Academy of Arts, and been a speaker at Gresham College. Festival performances include Lovebox and Bestival, and Festival Kometa in Riga, Latvia. Drawing on his background in both theatre and philosophy, his writing currently explores faith, relationships, and his overlapping identities.

He is a proud Barbican Young Poet alumnus, National Youth Theatre alumnus, and a former Roundhouse Resident Artist (2016-17) with Spit the Atom Poetry Collective.

At the Speed of Dark

Published by Bad Betty Press in 2020
www.badbettypress.com

Cover design by Amy Acre

Printed and bound in the United Kingdom

A CIP record of this book is available from the British Library.

ISBN: 978-1-913268-03-9

Supported using public funding by

**ARTS COUNCIL
ENGLAND**

LOTTERY FUNDED

At the
Speed
of
Dark

PRESS

At the Speed of Dark

Contents

when you come off Google Images and stick your head out the window

and winter is the result of naked trees, not their cause

and the sky is dark early

because this thing   passing through

takes all the white from the air right after noon

to take the vacuum of space with it.

but always forgets

the white flying up to meet it

is an answer to your prayers for release

you, in your bedroom

wonder if he has taken your brightness too.

maybe you've been reading it all wrong.

call this the spirit of taking and giving
        a sack
        a black hole
                scrap metal collector
                rag and bone thing;
                its vessel is not a comet,
                        just holy light trying to pass through cloud.
                        a smudge on a lens mistaken for a man.

you ask yourself how to deal with this darkness of days, turn on your desk lamp
as the candle light hops off the wick, dancing out of the room through the ceiling.
the sycamore at your window fingers the sky.
turn on your desk lamp, work through the darkness of day.
watch the bulb: stable thing, stretching flame in a snow globe rounded by its own gravity

Awe (n.) Definition II

i.
Seeing a body for the first time, meeting
a man at his funeral

staring him in the eyelid
his face is washed out.
Afro-European,
ashy brown.

You are waiting for him to breathe,
to end his cold, skinny nap,

then walking away.

ii.
Watching others weep in his presence.

You imagine they are not used to planting.
He probably needs watering, they think.

iii.
A young man stares
at the bloated white lining,
gleaming mahogany,
or the clothed stone wall beyond it,
crying from the fear of him.

iv.
The space between the eardrum
and the striking of a bell.

After My Name

After Sandra Cisneros

My name is a dodged Junior my father couldn't escape,
his Abayomi lodged in the heart of all his ID, and now his father's shade lives
in all he has tried to become.

In other people's mouths,
the name meaning   *the Lord is worthy of worship*   became *Toe San*.
Like an English speaker trying to honour a foot in broken Japanese.
I tire trying to hold my names for all their weight.
When I could finally pronounce them all,
it was a proclamation more about God and other persons
than myself

My father was going to call me Michael
(which is   *like El*   /   *who is like El*   /   *who is like El?*)
but a   Wòlíì   of the Celestial Church
at my naming ceremony said *[at most] he will be Gabriel*
instead (meaning   *strength of God*   /   *man of God*,   from
Gabor   or   *gibbor*,   for strongman or strength, and   *El*   for God.
That is,   *El is my strength*)
As though the seer knew I would not grow to be like God—I shouldn't
ask the question.

I still forget the order of my names,
think about which attribute
I'm growing furthest from. The strain
of all these titles on my neck is broadening my shoulders, making me
more a son of man each day, and every application form a sermon,
a chokehold—

*Notes on the Acknowledgements

When compiling this, I found an old version of the acknowledgements where I give thanks to *the love, presence and person of* [REDACTED].

This was always going to be past tense, whether [REDACTED] chose to stay present or not.
I ask myself whether it's best to keep, or cut [REDACTED] out, replace the name [REDACTED] with "[REDACTED]" wherever it appears in print.
After all, [REDACTED] lived in a corner of this volume. There is some of this that will always be for [REDACTED], just as the air in the workshop will always be a part of the pot, just as stray hairs or the potter's fingerprints stay in the clay.

Archaeologists use the patterns of wear on hip joints, the hardness of kneecaps, the gaps between teeth, and the bones of fingers and wrists to determine the sex and diet of dead things.

I can't remember the last thing we ate together.
This book's spine has [REDACTED]'s aftertaste in its marrow.

You ask about the things that dried but hadn't passed away

SEASON 20, EP. 5: CHILDHOOD.

JUMP CUT TO:

INT. BATHROOM - DAY. 2019

> ### NARRATOR (V.O.)
> When he reflects on his childhood, he finds he didn't
> enjoy it all that much and there's little to take away
> or talk about. Twenties Gabriel feels double his age
> without the wisdom, clout, or wholeness he'd hoped
> would come with growth.

CUT AWAY TO: FLASHBACK

INT. BEDROOM. THE OLD HOUSE - NIGHT. 2003. LIGHT
OFF. SLOW ZOOM ONTO BED.

> ### NARRATOR (V.O.)
> Maybe this old head is why his scalp thinks retirement
> is on the way. It would speak to his forehead and brow
> in hushed tones while he slept as a boy: talking about
> how they're

> ### SCALP
> worried about him

> ### NARRATOR (V.O.)
> again, and Eyebrows couldn't help but mention to
> Forehead that

EYEBROW 1

Gabriel has been staring at his hands

EYEBROW 2

and comparing them to his dad's.

SCALP

Remember when Gabriel soaked some cotton wool
and stuck it to Chin and pretended it was a beard?

FOREHEAD

And used a mop handle as a walking staff.

SCALP

All I want—

EYEBROWS

Sshhh. He's in REM sleep now

SCALP

All I want is for Gabriel to grow up gracefully.

EYEBROW 1

We've been trying,

EYEBROW 2

Really trying.

SCALP

But his dad's been shaving our—
wait—is there a bald spot? What's he trying to hide?!

FOREHEAD

He's *nine.*

EYEBROWS

SSHH.

SCALP (cont'd)

I feel like I'm fighting a lost cause.
He's always been the tallest in his class,
but the sky's getting closer these days,
white kids keep touching our hair,
and now part of my role's been split to the armpits;
it's only a matter of time before it's outsourced altogether.
Neck said Back's been thinking of a job share.
I'll explore my options. Maybe go part time. When he
graduates.

FADE OUT

Suspension

You cut through the white corridor joining Science and Drama,

faces expecting your fists to draw blood at the speed of dark.
Everything quakes

at your presence, air thick as a sea of reeds. Your hands are ready

to make another boy's face a tambourine for defiling your crown;

your afro a Byzantine halo: full and gleaming with fire.

24, thank god for life

you don't know what it means to celebrate a birthday any more,
opening gifts with a straight face.
you've forgotten how to respond to presents,
tried celebrating yourself and got bored.

another neighbour has cancer. a father is going for biopsies.
a 10am sky is liver-spotted, so pale its veins are showing,
congested, losing its hair.

you want to be something elsewhere.
a few weeks back snow fell when it shouldn't have.
today, another overcast spring.
your bedroom ceiling, speckled and stained from old leaks in the roof,
gives a sardonic *me again. sorry yeah.* your whole bed is lukewarm.
your eyes open kissing their teeth.

Yes. Fam.

Tonight, you arrive. On your entry he stops.
His knuckles to your chest say
when I needed you, you weren't here.
He wants to beat all his hurt into your marrow.
His fists blur with street lights,
trying to shake the shadow off.

He says the highs are the worst, he has no one
to share these moments with. He apologises.
It is one thing to have a void, another to be filled
and then torn open. Fam.

You want to lower yourself into others
but cause overflow, like a body entering a bath.

Laurie says there's a fissure in her chest her mother falls into.
What you hear is we are born of scars.
We all start as the inside of someone else.
Sometimes she talks like she is a white dwarf waiting to black hole herself.
Fam.

Tonight, you sit with another, break baklava, sip coffee like the Blood at 1am.
Pour him another cup.
He is questioning faith and purpose. Tells you

his heart's membrane almost collapsed itself again. That his mind keeps falling
into his stomach. Every confession is a hymn on loop his pastor has grown sick of. Fam.

All your friends are frayed and unstitching inside.
You think on your father's body saying this world has made enough versions of him.

COMPLAINING

After Terrance Hayes

If it wasn't for your constant moaning,
I may have taken you seriously. You ask me if oiling
engines would have been more worthwhile. There is still so long
for you to go, and you're stuck trying to be honest and plain
in your work, wondering if your lamp
is worth the match that failed to light it, mapping
your way through your mental list of excuses. Your peers are icons
not because they are valuable and you are a failing coin,
but because they are good at carrying on. Yet here you are, nailing
yourself to a spaghetti stick cross, impaling
your loins with a toothpick. Child, behave. Stop pretending your task is the mouth of a lion.

Wu Tang Name: Lion Midnight

After Elizabeth Bishop

It is three hours into the day
and instead of sleeping,
Lion Midnight washes his hair
with eucalyptus and peppermint, sits
cross-legged in the bathtub with the shower head, turns
the water to the hottest setting, and no matter how many times he washes
and repeats, there is still grease and oil and nine months of standing air in
his mane.

The last time he washed his hair like this:
the other side of single, kneeling,
upper torso swan-necked over a bucket of steam.
Tonight the water is less grey and brown than it was.

He reflects
on all the things he has to do tomorrow,
messages he's aired, the last time he was this soft,
the last pair of arms that properly carried his hair
and head
like this.

After Yoga with Adriene

1.   Think of how you balance yourself.

     Legs wobble, feet start to slip, you
     are no tower, your neck is more like
     a herd of llamas stumbling down a cliff face.

2.   Take a low downward dog
     (Adriene calls *puppy position*)

     nothing is aligned like you want it to be
     but you trust that one day you will
     trust your body. You move
     up into downward dog.

     Again, neck twisting to see the screen,
     check if you're doing it right.
     You are. Look down,
     feel muscles suddenly exist.

3.   Find your torso
     hanging loose,
     a deflated pregnancy of water balloons.
     This isn't your body

     again. You wonder how anyone could miss this,
     tell you that it's beautiful;
     how they can want this next to them,
     even when they can see it.

It must be what's on the inside

after all: your real body is desperate
to escape this soft, smothering cell.

4.   Exhale.

Your skin draws in too, with your hair.
Your penis has started to shrink into your body.
Plus it's cold,
but your genitals know
this thing on the outside isn't your real body.
Again, it's cold. Remember

the point of this is escape.
Misery is not a storm cloud or a loyal black dog.
It is the air turning to fog and cotton wool,
it is sprinting in a swimming pool of fat.
The you that emerges will be god-like
if it doesn't choke first.

on trying to write about blackness and being black as a black male author who doesn't know what blackness is but feels it needs to be fire and relatable and relevant and personal

at 3 am you're looking for something deep or heavy or sublime to say about the night and growing in your skin.

you have nothing.

spent so long trying to compare the dark to your skin, eyes
and tangling hair
that it turned blue on you
like the irish term for an african
a white man's bruised eye
the beginning of a bad joke

a link as tenuous as your links to chains or windrush
or the music you're told you listen to: *rap, bob marley,* or grime
or the ones you want to start to love but fear you don't know how to
the yórùba you taught yourself to speak in church
your need to reference death, bullets, and blades
estates you forgot you grew up on
or your non-violence, the weakness of british sun, your bones, babylon.

you notice the hue of the bleeding ink and think
maybe this is a good enough metaphor: i can't escape
            the colour of my text, the coltan in my phone
            the horror of blank sheets
    or

            i studied philosophy and found
            all the textbook pages were white as my notebook.

now you're thinking too much
and this faux-quirky, false irony is white too.

this is what paper and pressure does
when you have to speak of something you are but never felt was yours
from day one
when trying to draw yourself
the black crayon never felt right
you'd reach for the brown one every time.

Recording

a ò mọ ohun tó ń kojá — Yorùbá idiom

u godè!

    ugbob dey!

loops from an unseen mouth

        all i have to say is   Àmín

                    ugbob dey!

Agatha Moses' broken Hausa skips
into her Igbo-accented English.

        all i have to say is   (Àmín)

ungob dey!

                    ungob dey!

    from the backseat of the Zafira
Grandma's RP   sings what her Yorùbá ear
commands the words to be:

                    (Amen)

ugwo deh!

    "All I have to say is

      who goes there?"

                    ungob dey!

ugwo deh!

I mention something about the future and university

                    ( )

28

ugwob dey!

ugwob dey!

She replies,
"If I live that long."

all i have to say is

who goes there?

( )

( )

loops silently like a knotted cassette

I didn't know her absence would come so quickly.
True true she wouldn't see the next year.

( )

I've grown
into the habit of asking stupid questions of God the air.
Some ~~bright~~ afternoons

the sky blacks out for a half-second.

I think

I see an answer passing

when the sun flickers,
and no bird or plane in the cloudless sky is big enough to do this.

thank you lord

all i have ____ is

( )

everything to eyelid

After Kareem Parkins-Brown

According to Omar, I'm always in
conversation with God. I'm not sure

whether that makes me spiritual
or just a very good liar. I've learned
to convince myself of the things I
want others to believe. I am an actor
trapped in character long after the
curtain has dropped. I've always been
playing myself. The plans I make get
weaker by the word, every   *right now*
has morphed to   *by the end of the day*
become *ASAP* faded into an *as soon as
I think I can.* This version of adulthood
is eroding my integrity like time and
water do stones. I fear one day it will
shrink to a twinkle on the horizon,
the glint of a headtop polished bald.
My scalp shows the strands of me
I've weathered promising too much.
I'm learning to forgive myself, to
stop seeing this body as a mass of
unguided flesh.
                    I don't know whether
the silence that follows prayer is
nothing or angels putting me on hold.

A voice used to speak from heaven
in my dreams. Now they all feature
waking up to realise I'm still asleep.
In these lucid dreams I am trying to
fly but failing to get off the ground,
and God fades everything to eyelid
the moment I realise what is possible.

body weight

[REDACTED] said there was something oddly sexual about the way I washed
my feet after getting stuck in a mudflat on Cramond Island.

the tide had gone way out and I,
not knowing the sea, or how to swim,

ventured too far off shore.

it was marsh here, for this sand was not solid or ready to hold a body's weight.
I stepped too far and it swallowed my right foot,
sandal and all, every inch of sole sucked whole.
when stepping back, my left foot sank in its place.
everywhere was deep, and wet, and in walking back to harder ground
the shore refused
to let go.

I relate how I spent what felt like an hour rinsing my feet in pools between the pylons
by the causeway, shaking each foot, kneading straps to save the leather.
I don't mention how my feet filled each pool with clay, clouds
reclaiming time, clawing back at the clearness of sky.

Notes

'when you come off Google Images and stick your head out the window' is an ekphrastic response to *Frío (Invierno)/Cold (Winter)*, a symbolic painting by Spanish Surrealist artist, Remedios Varo, 1948.

In 'After Ny Name', the title 'Wòlíì' is Yórùba for 'prophet', a rank of clergy in the Cherubim and Seraphim Churches and Celestial Church of Christ.

'Yes. Fam.' contains a reference to 'Delicate' by Laurie Ogden, first published in *For Those with Collages for Tongues (2018)*. Written for DJSB, LEO, NGT, and BG.

The quasi-refrain of 'Recording' is taken from a refrain sung by Nigerian Gospel singer, Agatha Moses, from track two of her album, *Nigerian Praises*. The Yorùbá idiom, 'a ò mọ ohun tó ń kọjá', translates literally as 'we do not/one does not know what is passing'. The word 'ohun' can also be translated 'voice' if [mis]pronounced with different vowel tones.

Acknowledgements

'when you come off Google Images and stick your head out the window', 'Awe (n.) Definition II' and 'Suspension' were first published respectively in the Barbican Young Poets anthologies, *The Words for These Things* (2019), *Impossible Things About Optimism* (2016) and *For Those With Collages for Tongues* (2018).

'COMPLAINING' is written as a gramme of &s, a form devised by Terrance Hayes.

'Wu Tang Name: Lion Midnight' is written for RS, after 'The Shampoo' by Elizabeth Bishop and the Wu Tang Clan Name Generator sites of 2002 and 2019.

Thank you to all my friends, mentors, and unofficial editors from across the poetry scene and beyond; to everyone who helped make this a possibility, helped force this into being, and believed in me even when I didn't. Especially to the following:

To Amy Acre and Jake Wild Hall of Bad Betty Press for making (sure) this happened.

To Jacob Sam-La Rose, for everything. To Rachel Long and Kat Francois; Jeremiah Brown, Laurie Ogden, Bayan Goudarzpour, Theresa Lola, Troy Cabida, Eleanor Penny, Antonia Jade King, the Barbican Young Poets; everyone I've name-checked, and all I've written some of these poems after.

Thank you to Elizabeth, Raphael, and my parents.

New and recent titles from Bad Betty Press

War Dove
Troy Cabida

bloodthirsty for marriage
Susannah Dickey

poems for my FBI agent
Charlotte Geater

No Weakeners
Tim Wells

The Body You're In
Phoebe Wagner

Blank
Jake Wild Hall

*And They Are Covered
in Gold Light*
Amy Acre

Alter Egos
Edited by Amy Acre
and Jake Wild Hall

She Too Is a Sailor
Antonia Jade King

Raft
Anne Gill

While I Yet Live
Gboyega Odubanjo

The Death of a Clown
Tom Bland

Forthcoming in 2020

Animal Experiments
Anja Konig

A Terrible Thing
Gita Ralleigh

Sylvanian Family
Summer Young

Rheuma
William Gee